The Food and Drug Administration

KNOW YOUR GOVERNMENT

The Food and Drug Administration

William Patrick

CHELSEA HOUSE PUBLISHERS

Chelsea House Publishers
Editor-in-Chief: Nancy Toff
Executive Editor: Remmel T. Nunn
Managing Editor: Karyn Gullen Browne
Copy Chief: Juliann Barbato
Picture Editor: Adrian G. Allen
Manufacturing Manager: Gerald Levine

Know Your Government
Senior Editor: Kathy Kuhtz

Staff for THE FOOD AND DRUG ADMINISTRATION
Associate Editor: Pierre Hauser
Copy Editors: Richard Fumosa, Karen Hammonds
Deputy Copy Chief: Ellen Scordato
Editorial Assistant: Theodore Keyes
Picture Researcher: Anne Hobart
Assistant Art Director: Laurie Jewell
Designer: Noreen M. Lamb
Production Coordinator: Joseph Romano

3 5 7 9 8 6 4 2

Library of Congress Cataloging in Publication Data

Patrick, Bill.
  The Food and Drug Administration.
  (Know your government)
  Bibliography: p.
  Includes index.
  Summary: Surveys the history of the Food and Drug Administration, describing its structure, function, and influence on American society.
  1. United States. Food and Drug Administration. 2. Food adulteration and inspection—United States. 3. Pharmaceutical policy—United States. [1. United States. Food and Drug Administration. 2. Food adulteration and inspection. 3. Pharmaceutical policy]
  I. Title. II. Series: Know your government (New York, N.Y.)
  HD9000.9.U5P37   1988   353.0077'8   87-34121
  ISBN 0-87754-822-6
     0-7910-0865-7 (pbk.)

CONTENTS

KNOW YOUR GOVERNMENT

CHELSEA HOUSE PUBLISHERS

INTRODUCTION

Government: Crises of Confidence

Arthur M. Schlesinger, jr.

From the start, Americans have regarded their government with a mixture of reliance and mistrust. The men who founded the republic did not doubt the indispensability of government. "If men were angels," observed the 51st Federalist Paper, "no government would be necessary." But men are not angels. Because human beings are subject to wicked as well as to noble impulses, government was deemed essential to assure freedom and order.

At the same time, the American revolutionaries knew that government could also become a source of injury and oppression. The men who gathered in Philadelphia in 1787 to write the Constitution therefore had two purposes in mind. They wanted to establish a strong central authority and to limit that central authority's capacity to abuse its power.

To prevent the abuse of power, the Founding Fathers wrote two basic principles into the new Constitution. The principle of federalism divided power between the state governments and the central authority. The principle of the separation of powers subdivided the central authority itself into three branches—the executive, the legislative, and the judiciary—so that "each may be a check on the other." The *Know Your Government* series focuses on the major executive departments and agencies in these branches of the federal government.

The Constitution did not plan the executive branch in any detail. After vesting the executive power in the president, it assumed the existence of "executive departments" without specifying what these departments should be. Congress began defining their functions in 1789 by creating the Departments of State, Treasury, and War. The secretaries in charge of these departments made up President Washington's first cabinet. Congress also provided for a legal officer, and President Washington soon invited the attorney general, as he was called, to attend cabinet meetings. As need required, Congress created more executive departments.

Setting up the cabinet was only the first step in organizing the American state. With almost no guidance from the Constitution, President Washington, seconded by Alexander Hamilton, his brilliant secretary of the treasury, equipped the infant republic with a working administrative structure. The Federalists believed in both executive energy and executive accountability and set high standards for public appointments. The Jeffersonian opposition had less faith in strong government and preferred local government to the central authority. But when Jefferson himself became president in 1801, although he set out to change the direction of policy, he found no reason to alter the framework the Federalists had erected.

By 1801 there were about 3,000 federal civilian employees in a nation of a little more than 5 million people. Growth in territory and population steadily enlarged national responsibilities. Thirty years later, when Jackson was president, there were more than 11,000 government workers in a nation of 13 million. The federal establishment was increasing at a faster rate than the population.

Jackson's presidency brought significant changes in the federal service. He believed that the executive branch contained too many officials who saw their jobs as "species of property" and as "a means of promoting individual interest." Against the idea of a permanent service based on life tenure, Jackson argued for the periodic redistribution of federal offices, contending that this was the democratic way and that official duties could be made "so plain and simple that men of intelligence may readily qualify themselves for their performance." He called this policy rotation-in-office. His opponents called it the spoils system.

In fact, partisan legend exaggerated the extent of Jackson's removals. More than 80 percent of federal officeholders retained their jobs. Jackson discharged no larger a proportion of government workers than Jefferson had done a generation earlier. But the rise in these years of mass political parties gave federal patronage new importance as a means of building the party and of rewarding activists. Jackson's successors were less restrained in the distribution of spoils. As the federal establishment grew—to nearly 40,000 by 1861—the politicization of the public service excited increasing concern.

After the Civil War the spoils system became a major political issue. High-minded men condemned it as the root of all political evil. The spoilsmen, said the British commentator James Bryce, "have distorted and depraved the mechanism of politics." Patronage, by giving jobs to unqualified, incompetent, and dishonest persons, lowered the standards of public service and nourished corrupt political machines. Office-seekers pursued presidents and cabinet secretaries without mercy. "Patronage," said Ulysses S. Grant after his presidency, "is the bane of the presidential office." "Every time I appoint someone to office," said another political leader, "I make a hundred enemies and one ingrate." George William Curtis, the president of the National Civil Service Reform League, summed up the indictment. He said,

> The theory which perverts public trusts into party spoils, making public
> employment dependent upon personal favor and not on proved merit,
> necessarily ruins the self-respect of public employees, destroys the
> function of party in a republic, prostitutes elections into a desperate
> strife for personal profit, and degrades the national character by lower-
> ing the moral tone and standard of the country.

The object of civil service reform was to promote efficiency and honesty in the public service and to bring about the ethical regeneration of public life. Over bitter opposition from politicians, the reformers in 1883 passed the Pendleton Act, establishing a bipartisan Civil Service Commission, competitive examinations, and appointment on merit. The Pendleton Act also gave the president authority to extend by executive order the number of "classified" jobs—that is, jobs subject to the merit system. The act applied initially only to about 14,000 of the more than 100,000 federal positions. But by the end of the 19th century 40 percent of federal jobs had moved into the classified category.

Civil service reform was in part a response to the growing complexity of American life. As society grew more organized and problems more technical, official duties were no longer so plain and simple that any person of intelligence could perform them. In public service, as in other areas, the all-round man was yielding ground to the expert, the amateur to the professional. The excesses of the spoils system thus provoked the counter-ideal of scientific public administration, separate from politics and, as far as possible, insulated against it.

The cult of the expert, however, had its own excesses. The idea that administration could be divorced from policy was an illusion. And in the realm of policy, the expert, however much segregated from partisan politics, can

9

never attain perfect objectivity. He remains the prisoner of his own set of values. It is these values rather than technical expertise that determine fundamental judgments of public policy. To turn over such judgments to experts, moreover, would be to abandon democracy itself; for in a democracy final decisions must be made by the people and their elected representatives. "The business of the expert," the British political scientist Harold Laski rightly said, "is to be on tap and not on top."

Politics, however, were deeply ingrained in American folkways. This meant intermittent tension between the presidential government, elected every four years by the people, and the permanent government, which saw presidents come and go while it went on forever. Sometimes the permanent government knew better than its political masters; sometimes it opposed or sabotaged valuable new initiatives. In the end a strong president with effective cabinet secretaries could make the permanent government responsive to presidential purpose, but it was often an exasperating struggle.

The struggle within the executive branch was less important, however, than the growing impatience with bureaucracy in society as a whole. The 20th century saw a considerable expansion of the federal establishment. The Great Depression and the New Deal led the national government to take on a variety of new responsibilities. The New Deal extended the federal regulatory apparatus. By 1940, in a nation of 130 million people, the number of federal workers for the first time passed the 1 million mark. The Second World War brought federal civilian employment to 3.8 million in 1945. With peace, the federal establishment declined to around 2 million by 1950. Then growth resumed, reaching 2.8 million by the 1980s.

The New Deal years saw rising criticism of "big government" and "bureaucracy." Businessmen resented federal regulation. Conservatives worried about the impact of paternalistic government on individual self-reliance, on community responsibility, and on economic and personal freedom. The nation in effect renewed the old debate between Hamilton and Jefferson in the early republic, although with an ironic exchange of positions. For the Hamiltonian constituency, the "rich and well-born," once the advocate of affirmative government, now condemned government intervention, while the Jeffersonian constituency, the plain people, once the advocate of a weak central government and of states' rights, now favored government intervention.

In the 1980s, with the presidency of Ronald Reagan, the debate has burst out with unusual intensity. According to conservatives, government intervention abridges liberty, stifles enterprise, and is inefficient, wasteful, and arbitrary. It disturbs the harmony of the self-adjusting market and creates worse troubles than it solves. Get government off our backs, according to the popular cliché, and our problems will solve themselves. When government is necessary, let it be at the local level, close to the people. Above all, stop the inexorable growth of the federal government.

In fact, for all the talk about the "swollen" and "bloated" bureaucracy, the federal establishment has not been growing as inexorably as many Americans seem to believe. In 1949, it consisted of 2.1 million people. Thirty years later, while the country had grown by 70 million, the federal force had grown only by 750,000. Federal workers were a smaller percentage of the population in 1985 than they were in 1955—or in 1940. The federal establishment, in short, has not kept pace with population growth. Moreover, national defense and the postal service account for 60 percent of federal employment.

Why then the widespread idea about the remorseless growth of government? It is partly because in the 1960s the national government assumed new and intrusive functions: affirmative action in civil rights, environmental protection, safety and health in the workplace, community organization, legal aid to the poor. Although this enlargement of the federal regulatory role was accompanied by marked growth in the size of government on all levels, the expansion has taken place primarily in state and local government. Whereas the federal force increased by only 27 percent in the 30 years after 1950, the state and local government force increased by an astonishing 212 percent.

Despite the statistics, the conviction flourishes in some minds that the national government is a steadily growing behemoth swallowing up the liberties of the people. The foes of Washington prefer local government, feeling it is closer to the people and therefore allegedly more responsive to popular needs. Obviously there is a great deal to be said for settling local questions locally. But local government is characteristically the government of the locally powerful. Historically, the way the locally powerless have won their human and constitutional rights has often been through appeal to the national government. The national government has vindicated racial justice against local bigotry, defended the Bill of Rights against local vigilantism, and protected natural resources against local greed. It has civilized industry and secured the rights of labor organizations. Had the states' rights creed prevailed, there would perhaps still be slavery in the United States.

The national authority, far from diminishing the individual, has given most Americans more personal dignity and liberty than ever before. The individual freedoms destroyed by the increase in national authority have been in the main the freedom to deny black Americans their rights as citizens; the freedom to put small children to work in mills and immigrants in sweatshops; the freedom to pay starvation wages, require barbarous working hours, and permit squalid working conditions; the freedom to deceive in the sale of goods and securities; the freedom to pollute the environment—all freedoms that, one supposes, a civilized nation can readily do without.

"Statements are made," said President John F. Kennedy in 1963, "labelling the Federal Government an outsider, an intruder, an adversary. . . . The United States Government is not a stranger or not an enemy. It is the people of fifty states joining in a national effort. . . . Only a great national effort by a great people working together can explore the mysteries of space, harvest the products at the bottom of the ocean, and mobilize the human, natural, and material resources of our lands."

So an old debate continues. However, Americans are of two minds. When pollsters ask large, spacious questions—Do you think government has become too involved in your lives? Do you think government should stop regulating business?—a sizable majority opposes big government. But when asked specific questions about the practical work of government—Do you favor social security? unemployment compensation? Medicare? health and safety standards in factories? environmental protection? government guarantee of jobs for everyone seeking employment? price and wage controls when inflation threatens?—a sizable majority approves of intervention.

In general, Americans do not want less government. What they want is more efficient government. They want government to do a better job. For a time in the 1970s, with Vietnam and Watergate, Americans lost confidence in the national government. In 1964, more than three-quarters of those polled had thought the national government could be trusted to do right most of the time. By 1980 only one-quarter was prepared to offer such trust. But by 1984 trust in the federal government to manage national affairs had climbed back to 45 percent.

Bureaucracy is a term of abuse. But it is impossible to run any large organization, whether public or private, without a bureaucracy's division of labor and hierarchy of authority. And we live in a world of large organizations. Without bureaucracy modern society would collapse. The problem is not to abolish bureaucracy, but to make it flexible, efficient, and capable of innovation.

Two hundred years after the drafting of the Constitution, Americans still regard government with a mixture of reliance and mistrust—a good combination. Mistrust is the best way to keep government reliable. Informed criticism is the means of correcting governmental inefficiency, incompetence, and arbitrariness; that is, of best enabling government to play its essential role. For without government, we cannot attain the goals of the Founding Fathers. Without an understanding of government, we cannot have the informed criticism that makes government do the job right. It is the duty of every American citizen to know our government—which is what this series is all about.

Shoppers select apples in a supermarket produce department. Fresh fruits bearing excessive residues from insecticide sprays are considered to be contaminated under the Food, Drug, and Cosmetic Act of 1938.

ONE

Protecting the Consumer

How nutritious is the food that you buy in a supermarket? Is the nonprescription medicine that you purchase in a drugstore really effective? Does your sunscreen lotion actually block out the harmful rays of the sun? Does your television set emit too much radiation? These are some of the myriad issues that the Food and Drug Administration (FDA) deals with everyday to protect the health of consumers in the United States.

The FDA is an agency of the Public Health Service, a division of the U.S. Department of Health and Human Services. Its job is to enforce the Federal Food, Drug, and Cosmetic Act, passed in 1938 to ensure that foods are safe to eat, pure in quality, and produced under sanitary conditions. As part of its mission, the FDA regulates the manufacture and sale of drugs and cosmetics to make sure they are not harmful to consumers and are effective in their intended uses. The FDA develops standards for the composition, quality, nutrition, and safety of foods, food additives (substances added to improve desirability, such as flavors, colors, and preservatives), and cosmetics. The FDA monitors the safety of medical devices, such as thermometers and heart pacemakers, and veterinary preparations, such as livestock antibiotics. The FDA also conducts research programs to study the potentially poisonous effects of chemical substances that are in food, drugs, cosmetics, or the environment. FDA researchers try to determine the risks to humans from long-term, low-level exposure to the toxic compounds and establish guidelines that can be used in managing these risks.

The task of the FDA is complex and diversified. To meet its challenges the agency employs a host of experts: physicians, biologists, pharmacists, chemists, physicists, bacteriologists, and numerous other groups of scientists and technicians.

Members of the field staff serve as the "eyes and ears" of the FDA. Hundreds of technically trained FDA consumer safety officers, or inspectors, around the country are responsible for examining the output of the more than 100,000 businesses that manufacture or deal in products destined for "interstate," or between states, commerce. (State laws govern those businesses having only local dealings.) These consumer safety officers form the backbone of the FDA's enforcement program.

The basic philosophy of the FDA is to prevent violation of the health and safety laws passed by Congress. A great majority of food, drug, and cosmetic manufacturers act responsibly and believe in the concept that what is good for the consumer is also good for business. The FDA, therefore, can center its attention on those firms that act carelessly or unlawfully.

FDA consumer safety officers check an Israeli orange shipment for mercury contamination by running the fruit through a metal-detecting machine. Imported products regulated by the FDA are subject to inspection upon entry through U.S. Customs.

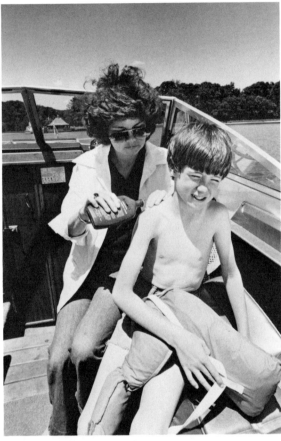

A mother puts sunscreen lotion on her son to help protect him against sunburn. The FDA defines sunscreen lotion as both a cosmetic and a drug because it is intended to prevent a skin disease—sun poisoning.

For centuries, people have been concerned about the food and drink that they put into their bodies. In early Egypt, strict laws regulated meat handling. In ancient Greece and Rome, the dilution of wine with water was specifically forbidden. During the Middle Ages, European merchants and apothecaries often banded together into guilds (associations), partly to protect their spices and drugs from being tampered with.

Today, the American public generally takes for granted that the food, drug, and cosmetic products it buys are safe; however, this was not always the case. History is riddled with incidents where hundreds of people became ill or died after ingesting poisonous foods or addictive drugs. Fortunately, improvements in manufacturing technologies and changes in federal food and drug laws have done a great deal to prevent similar tragedies from occurring over the past few decades.

Dr. Harvey Wiley, photographed in the Bureau of Chemistry laboratory in 1907, championed the crusade against impure food and fraudulent patent medicines. While he was chief chemist, Wiley conducted experiments that proved that some chemical preservatives were hazardous.

TWO

Early Food and Drug Laws

Although the Food and Drug Administration as we know it today was not established until 1906, efforts to regulate food and drugs in the United States began long ago. In the colonies, local food laws were passed to regulate the weight of loaves of bread baked commercially. These laws, called "assizes of bread," established a standard weight for loaves that was in relation to the current price of wheat and flour. Essentially, these laws fixed prices by regulating the profit of the middleman and baker, but leaving the price of grain open to fluctuate with the market. In 1646, the Massachusetts Bay Colony ordered every baker to use a distinct mark for his bread and keep the assize of the loaves as had been established by law. Inspectors were chosen and given authority to enter bakeries and weigh bread to assure that the law was being obeyed. Bakers who were found to be cheating the public were required to surrender their goods to the inspector, who would keep a third of the bread for himself—as payment for his time—and give the rest to the poor. The colonies enacted numerous food inspection laws to establish standard weights and measures, including the sizes of casks and barrels used to store and ship foods such as fish, pork, beef, and flour. These laws often reflected the significance of a particular industry to each colony's economy: Massachusetts had strict

19

Mexican Treacheries and Cruelties.

INCIDENTS AND SUFFERINGS
IN THE
MEXICAN WAR;
WITH

Accounts of Hardships endured; Treacheries of the Mexicans; Battles Fought, and Success of American Arms;

The "Heroine of Fort Brown."

Also, an Account of Valiant Soldiers Fallen,
AND THE PARTICULARS OF THE
Death and Funeral Services in honor of
Capt. George Lincoln, of Worcester.

BY A VOLUNTEER RETURNED FROM THE WAR.

BOSTON AND NEW YORK:
1847.

Entered according to Act of Congress, in the year 1847, by LIEUT. G. N. ALLEN.

Dealers supplied at HALL'S, 66 Cornhill, Boston.

On an 1847 broadside U.S. soldiers drink quinine water during the Mexican War. It was later discovered that the water, given to treat malaria, was poisoned. The Import Drugs Act was passed in 1848 to protect the United States from contaminated foreign food and drugs.

laws governing fishing, its foremost industry; New York had tough regulations for the beef industry; and Virginia and Maryland regulated their tobacco industry carefully.

In 1785, Massachusetts enacted the nation's first general food law. "Be it therefore enacted," read the act, "that any person selling diseased, corrupted, contagious, or unwholesome provisions, whether for meat or drink . . . shall be punished by fine, imprisonment, standing in the pillory or one or more of these punishments." Many other states passed similar legislation in the decades that followed. In general, however, these laws were legally vague, weakly enforced, and did little to cut down on what was becoming an increasing problem: impure or contaminated food.

The earliest federal regulation of products for human consumption began in 1848. That year the Import Drugs Act was passed, following the discovery that some Mexican quinine water given to U.S. troops to treat malaria was contaminated and led to the death of some of the soldiers. The new law required laboratory inspections at the port of entry for imported drugs and allowed the holding, destruction, or refusal of cargoes that did not meet the standards described in the pharmacopoeia (the reference book in the United States designating the properties, actions, uses, dosages of, and standards of strength and purity for drugs), first published in 1820. The Import Drugs Act was the first in a long series of laws designed to protect U.S. consumers from the importation of impure and unsafe food and drugs.

Such legislation, however, was directed at controlling foreign products. Unfortunately, in the United States, the last half of the 19th century saw an increasing amount of domestic goods being manufactured and sold under less than honest and sanitary conditions. This was particularly true of food products such as meat, butter, and milk.

Workers drag a dead cow from the stable directly after it was milked. This 1858 engraving characterizes conditions of the milk trade in New York before there were state and local regulations.

There were several reasons for the deterioration of goods. The United States at this time was increasingly becoming an industrial rather than an agrarian society. As more and more people lived congested in towns and cities and were thus unable to grow their own food, the reliance on distant markets for food supplies grew. New railroads and other improvements in transportation facilities, along with packaging and manufacturing advancements, permitted larger amounts of food to be distributed over wider areas. Competition in sales often became intense and tempted some companies to adulterate (make impure) or mislabel their products to increase profits or to stay in business.

In the final decades of the 19th century, many cases of adulterated or mislabeled foods were reported. So-called butter was regularly laced with heavy amounts of lard, a fat obtained from hogs. Dangerous chemical preservatives such as boric acid were commonly used in many food products. Items labeled "potted chicken" would often contain no chicken whatsoever. One study conducted by the Department of Agriculture found that 90 percent of the "Vermont maple syrup" sold in the nation was actually from other states.

By 1900, the drug and cosmetic industries were in just as bad a condition. Thousands of so-called patent medicines flooded the market. Seemingly

Grain transported by rail to an elevator in New York City in 1877. As cities grew in size, they depended more and more on distant markets for food supplies. The contamination of food during transport and storage increasingly became a problem.

An array of late-19th-century patent medicines that claimed to cure all pains and various aches. Consumers were fooled by the false claims of these products and often became addicted to the harmful drugs they contained.

anyone who could pour two chemicals into a jar was marketing the concoction as a cure-all for every conceivable illness. Over-the-counter medicines containing highly addictive drugs such as morphine and heroin were openly sold. Many baby products that promised a good night's sleep contained cocaine (then a misunderstood and legal drug). So, too, did many leading cough syrups; none of these products displayed warning labels.

As an increasing number of people became addicted to what they thought were medicines and poisoned by what they expected to be wholesome food, more and more scientists and social reformers campaigned for changes in the nation's food and drug laws. Lawmakers began to face heightened pressure to stand up to those businesses that valued money more than the health of their customers.

As a result of the growing agitation, no fewer than 190 legislative measures dealing with the adulteration and mislabeling of food and drugs were introduced into the U.S. Congress between 1879 and 1906. However, not one of these bills was passed by Congress, which refused to support food and drug legislation.

The so-called poison squad, a group of volunteers who agreed to eat chemical preservatives to determine their effects on health. Dr. Wiley's experiments lasted from 1902 to 1907 and convinced the public that some preservatives could be harmful and should rarely be used in food.

According to Dr. Harvey Wiley, the chief chemist of the U.S. Department of Agriculture from 1883 to 1912, opposition to federal pure food legislation was threefold. In his revealing autobiography, Wiley wrote, "In the first instance, opposition came from those who thought such legislation an infringement of the police powers of the various states; secondly, it was opposed by those who failed to grasp the serious nature of the problem; and, finally, it was fought by interests who saw in its passage the termination of lucrative business practices."

Among the latter group, Wiley blamed the manufacturers who used dangerous preservatives to prolong the shelf life of the food they marketed; the makers of those harmful preservatives and adulterants; the producers of fake whiskey, which was made of nothing more than alcohol and coloring; the patent medicine manufacturers with their quack remedies for serious illnesses; and, in general, anybody unscrupulous enough to make money by mislabeling or contaminating food and drug products.

Wiley's observations were quite accurate; in fact, much can be learned about the history of food and drug laws in the United States by studying his remarkable career. A Harvard-trained son of an Indiana minister, Wiley was for more than two decades the leading spokesman for strong federal pure-food and drug laws. In 1883, he left his teaching position at Purdue University to become the head of the Bureau of Chemistry in the U.S. Department of Agriculture. Until that time, most chief chemists had been content to circulate periodic, scientific bulletins on issues that had little impact on society. Wiley would soon begin to change all that.

When he became head of the Bureau of Chemistry, Wiley had only two lab assistants and a secretary to help him. Working out of a solitary basement room in the Department of Agriculture building, Wiley immediately began to reorganize and build up his division. He quickly recruited and trained scientists and inspectors to assist him on what would soon become a crusade against malpractices in the food and drug industries.

With conditions as bad as they were in these industries, Wiley and his staff had no difficulty digging up juicy information for the division's reports and bulletins. Unlike most of his predecessors, Wiley took his findings directly to the public. He was frequently invited to lecture to women's clubs, health organizations, and businesspeople.

In 1903, Wiley shocked the nation by setting up a volunteer "poison squad." This group of young men agreed to eat foods containing measured amounts of chemical preservatives to see whether they proved hazardous to health. Although several of the volunteers did experience minor health problems, the experiment helped popularize Wiley's overall efforts. There were even songs written about the poison squad. The chorus from one of them went as follows:

O, they may get over it but they'll never look the same,
That kind of bill of fare would drive most men insane.
Next week he'll give them mothballs, a la Newburgh or else plain:
O, they may get over it but they'll never look the same.

In the end, the five-year experiment convinced the public that chemical preservatives should be used with utmost caution, if at all.

For years, Wiley had pleaded with Congress to initiate reforms in the food and drug industries, and his entreaties had been ignored; but public sentiment was turning, thanks largely to the efforts of thousands of women activists.

During the last quarter of the 19th century they, like Wiley, had been lobbying for a federal food and drug law. Although women could not vote at that time, their outraged demands were being increasingly heeded by politicians.

Another event also prodded Congress to speed up passage of long overdue legislation: the publication in 1905 of Upton Sinclair's widely read novel *The Jungle*. Sinclair pointed a provocative and accusatory finger at the meat industry. The following is a passage from his famous exposé:

> There was never the least attention paid to what was cut up for the sausage; there would come all the way back from Europe old sausage that had been rejected, and that was moldy and white—it would be doused with borax and glycerine, and dumped into the hoppers, and made over again for home consumption. There would be meat that had tumbled out on the floor in the dirt and sawdust, where the workers had tramped and spit uncounted billions of consumption germs. There would be meat stored in great piles and thousands of rats would race over it. It was too dark in those storage areas for a man to see well, but a man could run his hand over these piles of meat and sweep off handfuls of the dried dung of rats. These rats were nuisances, and the packers would put poisoned bread out for them; they would die, and then rats, bread, and meat would go into the hoppers together.

The American public was rightfully disgusted after reading Sinclair's graphic but realistic disclosures. In fact, almost overnight, sales of meat and meat products declined by 50 percent. Added pressure was put on Congress to take

Men prepare skins in the sausage department of a Chicago meat packing plant in 1893. The deplorable and insanitary conditions seen here and in similar plants were graphically described in Sinclair Lewis's 1905 novel The Jungle.

President Theodore Roosevelt supported Dr. Wiley's efforts to regulate food and drug manufacturing. In 1906, he signed the Food and Drugs Act, which prohibited interstate commerce of mislabeled and contaminated foods, drinks, and drugs.

action. Even the wounded meat industry recognized that government regulations could mean renewed sales. In his message to Congress on December 5, 1905, President Theodore Roosevelt strongly urged passage of new food and drug laws.

Finally, on June 30, 1906, Congress passed the first federal Pure Food and Drugs Act, according to which it became a federal crime to mislabel or adulterate foods, drinks, and drugs intended for interstate commerce.

The provisions of the law were to be enforced by the Bureau of Chemistry in the Department of Agriculture. Wiley was appointed by Secretary of Agriculture James Wilson to administer and enforce the landmark legislation—the cornerstone of the future Food and Drug Administration.

A Bureau of Chemistry inspector checks the quality of spinach at a spinach cannery in 1915. Behind him workers pack spinach into tin cans.

THREE

The Birth and Growth of the FDA

The Pure Food and Drugs Act of 1906 was, without a doubt, an immense benefit to the American consumer. It provided for 32 years the major protection against the adulteration and misbranding, or mislabeling, of food and drugs. In addition, the experience its administrators gained in carrying out its provisions proved most helpful in writing later food and drug laws.

What did the 1906 act actually do? First, it included a glossary of terms that defined precisely what was meant by words such as "food," "misbranding," and "adulteration." For example, food was defined to include all substances used for food, drink, or seasoning for human or animal consumption. A food was considered adulterated in the following instances:

1. If something was added to reduce its quality or strength.
2. If any substance had been substituted for the product.
3. If an important part of the food had been removed in any way.
4. If its damaged condition was hidden in any way.
5. If any poisonous ingredient had been added to make it dangerous to health.
6. If it contained any filthy substance or was the product of a diseased animal.

A food was considered misbranded if its label bore any false or misleading statements or if it was misrepresented by its package.

Wiley began administering the new law with no background in legal matters and with only a small staff of scientists to help him. In 1907, civil service examinations were first given to potential inspectors. Although more than 2,000 people took the test, only 28 inspectors were hired to cover the entire country. From this original group, Wiley selected as chief inspector Walter Campbell, a lawyer and an early advocate of consumer protection. (Campbell would enforce the nation's food and drug laws for a longer period of time than any other person.)

Under Wiley's supervision, the staff of the Bureau of Chemistry developed better scientific methods of analysis for food and drug protection. They refined legal procedures and methods of inspection and used them in hundreds of court battles, winning decisions that helped to fortify the new law.

Unfortunately, Wiley's enforcement years were stormy. He fought to ban the preservative sodium benzoate from catsup, saccharin from canned corn,

Barrels of contaminated salt fish and bags of tainted animal feed are seized by the Bureau of Chemistry in 1910. These foods were taken to a crematory and destroyed.

Mr. Walter Campbell (left) and Dr. Harvey Wiley in 1910. Together, these two men streamlined the methods of inspection used by the Bureau of Chemistry and worked to persuade Congress to amend the 1906 law.

and sulphur dioxide from dried fruit. But he was bitterly opposed by many of the industries it was his job to regulate. Also, people within the Department of Agriculture resented what they thought were his bullying tactics in carrying out the law. Farmers and processors complained about Wiley to such an extent that President Theodore Roosevelt set up review committees to curb the chief chemist's independent activities. Disappointed and resentful, Wiley resigned in 1912. Despite these problems, one historian of America's food and drug laws has written: "All in all, there never was, before or since in so short a time, such an extensive revolution within the food industries as took place between 1907 and 1912. Never since have conditions in the food industries been nearly as bad as those existing before the pure-food law of 1906 became effective."

Wiley was irritated by his inability to get Congress to pass a bill amending and strengthening the 1906 law. As important as it was, the Pure Food and

Federal inspectors examine sheep as they are pulled along a trolley in a Chicago meat plant. The Food and Drugs Act prohibited the processing of unhealthy animals and the use of toxic preservatives.

Drugs Act contained many loopholes. Although the Bureau of Chemistry could inspect food-processing plants and publish the findings of its investigations, it did not have the power to impose fines or penalties. In 1917, Dr. Carl Alsberg, who succeeded Wiley as chief chemist, pointed out in his annual report some limitations in the act:

> Especially conspicuous are the lack of legal standards for foods, of authority to inspect warehouses, and of any restriction whatever upon the use of many of the most virulent poisons in drugs; the limitations on the term "drug" by definition which make it difficult to control injurious cosmetics, fraudulent mechanical devices used for therapeutic purposes, as well as fraudulent remedies for obesity and leanness. . . . Furthermore, the law fails to cover fraudulent statements in advertising that are not in or on the food or drug package.

Technological and marketing advances were also soon making the 1906 law obsolete. In 1913, Congress enacted the Gould Amendment, which required quantity information on all food packages. And in 1914, in *U.S. v. Lexington*

Mill and Elevator Company, the Supreme Court ruled that the 1906 act did not require the government to prove that foods containing harmful substances *will* affect the public health, only that these substances *may* affect it. Nevertheless, for two decades following passage of the Pure Food and Drugs Act, there was little public pressure for a comprehensive amendment to the existing legislation. This apparent apathy was largely a result of the public's misguided faith in the 1906 act.

Unfortunately, the adulteration of foods continued. The 1906 act was so vague that judges often had difficulty upholding the standards that the Bureau of Chemistry had established. As a result, many manufacturers got away with unscrupulous practices. One example of industry misbranding during this period involved products labeled fruit jams that contained nothing more than water, sugar, and artificial coloring.

In 1921, Walter Campbell succeeded Dr. Alsberg as chief chemist of the Bureau of Chemistry and continued the fight against those in industry who abused the law. Campbell, who had been an ardent advocate of Wiley's enforcement policy, took over in 1924 all regulatory work of the bureau.

Once again, it took the publication of a book to swell public interest in more stringent food and drug laws. This time it was *Your Money's Worth. A Study in the Waste of the Consumer's Dollar*, by Stuart Chase and F. J. Schlink. Published in 1927, the book disclosed a number of frauds and urged the formation of consumer-supported testing clubs. Deceptions exposed in the study included fraudulent claims by manufacturers of fat reducers, mouthwashes, and toothpastes; cases of skin poisoning caused by hair dyes, face bleaches, face creams, and hair tonics; solvents, like tetrachloride, that were supposed to dissolve grease, kill moths, extinguish fires, and also be used as bath salts; and adulterated ingredients such as glue in gelatin, peas and rice hulls in coffee, and bacteria in catsup. One direct result of the book's publication was the creation of an organization called Consumers' Research, one of the earliest consumer groups to provide information to the public about the effectiveness of brand name products. (Within just a few years, the organization's membership grew from 1,000 to 45,000.)

Despite renewed consumer interest in strengthening the Pure Food and Drugs Act, no further legislation was passed until 1927, when Congress created the Food, Drug, and Insecticide Administration (FDIA) as a separate law-enforcement agency within the Department of Agriculture. Until then, funds to regulate the act were diverted from the budget allotted for research, making it increasingly difficult to conduct food tests. The secretary of agriculture hoped that by separating the administrative functions of research and enforcement into two divisions, Congress would increase appropriations for each. Campbell became the FDIA's first chief and, in 1931, the agency was renamed the Food and Drug Administration (FDA), the name it still has today.

The new Food and Drug Administration did much to reawaken concern over unhealthy and fraudulent food and drugs. It regularly broadcast radio programs to educate the nation on such issues as nutrition and health. The FDA also opened its department to independent writers to help them research and prepare articles on FDA-related topics.

Public interest in pure food and drugs was heightened even further by the Great Depression, which devastated the country in the 1930s. It was a time of great economic hardship for millions of Americans, most of whom wanted to make sure they got true value for every penny spent—and certainly on such essential items as food and drugs.

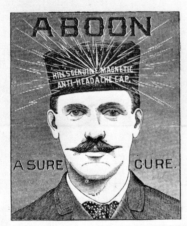

An advertisement for Hill's "genuine magnetic anti-headache cap," a fake medical device, exploited the new phenomenon of electricity and deceived trusting customers who ordered the device by mail. The 1906 law was powerless to control mail fraud, and swindlers escaped regulation until 1938.

A 1909 magazine cartoon ridicules the cosmetics and patent-medicine industries that were regulated by the Bureau of Chemistry.

President Franklin D. Roosevelt, who took office in 1933 pledging a "New Deal" for his beleaguered countrymen, was very concerned about consumer protection. After listening to convincing arguments by Campbell and Assistant Secretary of Agriculture Rexford Tugwell, Roosevelt—just months after becoming president—pushed for a total revision of the 1906 Food and Drugs Act.

For five years a bitter debate raged. On one side were FDA officials and consumer-minded congressmen favoring a strong new law; on the other were the leaders of the powerful advertising and manufacturing industries who would be most affected by new legislation.

Congress was deadlocked. In fact, it took a national catastrophe to get the two sides to compromise. This occurred in 1937 when a medicine concocted to treat sore throats ("elixir of sulfanilamide") was marketed without being properly tested for safety. As a result, 107 people died from what turned out to be a highly poisonous compound. Once again an outraged public called for reform. And once again organized women's clubs spearheaded the demand for new legislation. On June 25, 1938, President Roosevelt signed into law the Federal Food, Drug, and Cosmetic (FDC) Act. It was a major improvement over the 1906 act and remains to this day the basic food and drug law of the United States.

The FDC Act contained more than 40 major provisions that made it more powerful than the 1906 act. Among them were

1. Extending coverage to include cosmetics and therapeutic devices (devices such as heating pads and back braces).
2. Requiring drug companies to prove by scientific means that new drugs were safe before they could be distributed to the public.
3. Prohibiting the addition of poisonous substances to food except for unavoidable instances, in which it established maximum levels for these substances—for example, traces of pesticides.
4. Authorizing factory inspections.
5. Establishing food standards relating to quality and identity "to promote honesty and fair dealing in the interest of consumers."
6. Allowing court injunctions as a means of enforcing the law.
7. Proving fraud was no longer necessary for the FDA to stop a manufacturer from making untrue statements about a drug's effectiveness.

This comprehensive new law gave the FDA the tools it needed to better safeguard the nation's health. The act required packages of drugs to be labeled with ample warnings and adequate directions for use and prohibited the sale of those drugs found to be dangerous when used as directed. New drugs that were approved by the FDA were labeled for sale by prescription only. Familiar over-the-counter drugs were exempted from the required labels detailing directions for use. Distribution of dangerous drugs identified with what was called the Rx legend—"Caution: to be used only by or on the prescription of a————" (the blank was to be filled in with the word physician, dentist, or veterinarian)—could now be controlled through professional medical channels.

Yet problems persisted and, in some areas, multiplied. With the arrival of World War II another great technological leap took place. During wartime, scientific research and discovery accelerated at a dizzying pace. By the mid-1940s, a vast number of new drugs—especially antibiotics such as penicillin—and a wide variety of chemical compounds had been introduced. The FDA did its best to test thoroughly all new drugs that were rapidly being developed. It could not, however, keep up with the myriad chemical compounds that were increasingly being added to food products.

To deal with this problem, FDA commissioner Paul Dunbar, who succeeded Campbell in 1944, appealed to Congress in 1949. There he persuaded Representative Frank Keefe of Wisconsin to introduce a resolution to investigate all chemicals in food products, and later, in cosmetics as well. A House select committee on chemicals in foods and cosmetics, chaired by Representative James Delaney of New York, began two years of extensive hearings to study possible amendments to the 1938 law.

Over the next decade, the findings of the congressional investigations led to the enactment of three important amendments to the Food, Drug, and Cosmetic Act: the Miller Pesticide Amendment (1954), the Food Additives Amendment (1958), and the Color Additive Amendments (1960).

According to FDA historian Wallace Janssen, these amendments produced revolutionary changes. "With these laws on the books," he wrote, "it could be said for the first time that no substance can legally be introduced into the United States food supply unless there has been a prior determination that it is safe. By requiring the manufacturers to do the research a problem of unmanageable size was made manageable."

In short, the Miller Pesticide Amendment simplified the procedures used by the FDA to set reasonable limits on the amounts of pesticides permitted in agricultural products. The Food Additives Amendment prohibited the use of all

Bottles of Elixir Sulfanilamide, an alleged remedy for sore throats that was really a poisonous solvent. The concoction, which caused the death of more than a hundred people, had not been properly tested before being put on the market.

Michigan farmers spray an apple crop with insecticide in 1934. Until the Federal Food, Drug, and Cosmetic Act was passed in 1938, no standards for acceptable tolerances of pesticides in foods had been established.

food additives until the producer had scientifically proven their safety. The Color Additive Amendments permitted the FDA to regulate the conditions of safe use for color additives in food, drugs, and cosmetics. And like the Food Additives Amendment, they required that the manufacturers themselves perform the necessary scientific testing of additives to assure their safety.

Both the 1958 and 1960 amendments also contained another important and controversial provision; namely, that no additives of any sort would be considered safe if they had been found to be carcinogenic (carrying a cancer agent) during laboratory testing of animals. This provision, known as the

Delaney Clause, was so restrictive that it was opposed even by the FDA and many scientists. Opponents believed that some additives cause cancer in animals only at such high doses that it would be unreasonable to assume that the minuscule amounts in the actual product could cause cancer in humans. Those favoring the clause argued that no one has ever been able to determine what is a "safe" level for any carcinogenic substance.

The Delaney Clause became the basis for a 1959 FDA decision to recall all cranberries in the nation that had been treated with aminotriazole, a weed killer commonly used by cranberry growers. In December of that year, FDA chemists worked around the clock to test samples from nearly every cranberry crop in the country. Many thought this action was a bit extreme—newspaper editorialists and cartoonists poked fun at the FDA and gave it some negative publicity—but the recall conveyed the dangers of pesticides to farmers.

Earlier in the decade, the FDA had also drawn widespread attention and more positive publicity when it exposed a horsemeat scandal.

Early in 1950, state authorities in Illinois began to suspect that horsemeat was being substituted for beef in some of that state's meat markets and restaurants. Further investigation revealed that a ring of horsemeat racketeers extended all the way from Illinois to Florida and Texas. As more states became concerned and public alarm grew, it became necessary for state law-enforcement agencies to prove that suspect products were indeed horse-meat. Because beef and horsemeat are similar in taste and color, a foolproof test was essential to make the criminal charges stand up in court. Most state laboratories of the time lacked the sophisticated equipment needed for the test; as a result, the FDA was flooded with samples of alleged horsemeat. The agency's up-to-date devices for detecting adulteration were easily able to distinguish between the two meats. In the 2-year period from 1950 to 1952, more than 1,200 pieces of meat were sent to the FDA and nearly 25 percent proved to be horsemeat.

In 1956, William Randall of the FDA's Division of Antibiotics wrote, "During the course of these investigations a curious fact emerged—the vast majority of the American people do not like to eat horsemeat. During the horse racing season at Laurel, Maryland, it was announced in the newspapers that a Baltimore firm was selling hot dogs containing horsemeat. Consumption that day dropped from 40,000 to 40!" Clearly, concluded Randall, "it is the temper of the American public to bet on or ride horses, not to eat them."

The racketeers could no longer fool the public and were soon put out of business. Today it may be safely assumed that in the United States the misrepresentation of meat products is rare.

The passage of the food and color additives amendments marked the beginning of a trend toward *prevention* rather than only *punishment* for food and drug violations. In the early 1960s, that old adage "an ounce of prevention is worth a pound of cure" seemed to be the working slogan of lawmakers and scientists interested in improved food and drug laws. A medical tragedy in western Europe caused a public uproar for regulatory amendments to expand the scope of the FDC Act.

During the 1950s, the drug thalidomide appeared on the European market. This drug, supposedly a safe sedative and antiemetic (a medicine that prevents vomiting), was often prescribed for pregnant women. In 1960, an American

In 1943, a chemist at a manufacturing plant analyzes a sample of vi-
tamin B1, now called thiamine, to determine its chemical properties.
The Food, Drug, and Cosmetic Act required manufacturers to prove
the nutritional quality of vitamins, minerals, and proteins.

A woman applies lipstick to her lips. With the exception of color additives and a few other prohibited ingredients such as mercury compounds, a cosmetics manufacturer may use almost any raw material as a cosmetic ingredient and market the product without FDA approval.

pharmaceutical company requested permission from the FDA to market the drug in the United States. Dr. Frances O. Kelsey, a medical officer in the FDA's Division of New Drugs, was assigned to process the company's application and review its testing results. She was not satisfied with the company's initial data and asked for additional evidence of the drug's safety.

Meanwhile, doctors in Europe were making a horrifying discovery—thousands of pregnant women who had been taking thalidomide had given birth to deformed babies. Only Kelsey's concern for a detailed analysis of thalidomide had kept the drug off the American market and saved newborns in the United States from suffering a similar fate.

Finally, in the fall of 1962, Congress passed the Kefauver-Harris Drug Amendments. For the first time, drug manufacturers were required to prove to the FDA that new drugs were *effective* as well as safe before marketing them. The new law also specified that drug companies must send reports to the FDA telling of any adverse reactions experienced by users. Furthermore, they were required to inform doctors in their advertising material of the risks, as

FDA investigator Dr. Frances Kelsey testifies before the Senate's Government Operations Subcommittee in 1962 in support of the Kefauver-Harris Drug Amendments. Dr. Kelsey's demand for further testing of the drug thalidomide in 1960 prevented its distribution in the United States and thereby saved the country from the tragedy witnessed in Europe.

well as the benefits, of their drugs. Since the enactment of the amendments thousands of drugs have been removed from pharmacy shelves because they were not proven safe or effective. In summing up the effect of this legislation, Janssen claims that it was "one of the major advances in medical history."

Another amendment was required to strengthen the Food, Drug, and Cosmetic Act of 1938. During the 1960s, more and more Americans, especially young people, were using and abusing harmful drugs. In response to the increased misuse of drugs, in 1965 Congress passed the Drug Abuse Control Amendments. These were aimed at dealing with problems caused by three groups of dangerous drugs—depressants such as heroin, stimulants such as amphetamine, and hallucinogens such as lysergic acid diethylamide (LSD). The law allowed the FDA to seize illegal supplies of drugs, to serve warrants (documents that authorize an action, such as a search or an arrest), to arrest violators, and to require that all legal drug handlers keep exact records of all their supplies and sales.

In another move to combat drug abuse, the FDA's Bureau of Drug Abuse Control, established in 1966, was transferred in 1968 to the newly created Bureau of Narcotics and Dangerous Drugs in the Department of Justice. This consolidation made it easier to police the traffic of illegal drugs. It also meant that criminal investigations became a minor field of activity for the FDA itself.

However, although the FDA's role in policing drugs lessened during this period, the agency expanded into other areas. In 1960, thousands of chemical products intended for home use came under the control of the FDA when Congress passed the federal Hazardous Substances Labeling Act. The law

A customer enjoys oysters at a restaurant raw bar. Since 1968, the FDA has regulated the shellfish industry to protect consumers from shellfish harvested from polluted bodies of water.

required clear and prominent warning labels on all such products, whether hair spray or laundry detergent. In 1970, the FDA established a Bureau of Product Safety to administer the Hazardous Substances Labeling Act and subsequent home safety and accident prevention programs.

Because of a departmental reorganization in 1968, the FDA acquired several major health programs from other divisions of the Public Health Service. Among its new responsibilities were

1. Assuring the safety of milk supplies by working closely with state and local milk supply authorities.

2. Ensuring that shellfish not be harvested from polluted waters.

3. Guaranteeing that travelers on trains, buses, ships, and planes receive safe food and drink.

4. Promoting sanitary practices in restaurants and other establishments serving food.

5. Protecting victims of accidental poisoning by supplying poison control centers with the information needed for emergency treatment.

Two other important pieces of legislation that fell under the supervision of the FDA in the 1960s were the Child Protection Act (1966) and the Radiation Health and Safety Act (1968). The former banned from interstate commerce all hazardous toys intended for children, as well as all articles so dangerous that adequate warnings could not even be written for them. The purpose of the radiation law was to protect consumers from exposure to harmful amounts of radiation from electronic products and medical equipment. Radiation-emitting items such as television sets, microwave ovens, word processors, and X-ray equipment now had to be carefully checked by the FDA's Bureau of Radiological Health before being permitted on the market.

In 1976, the Medical Device Amendments were passed to revise and extend the 1938 FDC Act to provide greater consumer protection. Under the amendments, a device is specified as any health-care product that does not achieve any of its intended purposes by chemical action in or on the body or by being metabolized (the process by which substances are assimilated in the body). Such devices include thermometers, tongue depressors, intrauterine contraceptive devices, heart pacemakers, and kidney dialysis machines. The regulations require that manufacturers register with the FDA, explain the products they produce, and follow certain quality control procedures.

In 1980, Congress passed the Instant Formula Act after an outbreak of a serious illness affecting babies was traced to a mineral deficiency in some baby formulas. Two years later, the nation was stunned to learn about a rash of deaths caused by someone putting cyanide, a deadly poison, in Extra-Strength Tylenol pain relief capsules. The FDA quickly drew up regulations requiring that all such products be sold in tamper-resistant packages. And in 1983, the Anti-Tampering Act made it a crime to tamper with packaged consumer products.

In recent years, the FDA has been increasingly criticized for its sluggish approval of new drugs that preliminary tests show might be beneficial to many

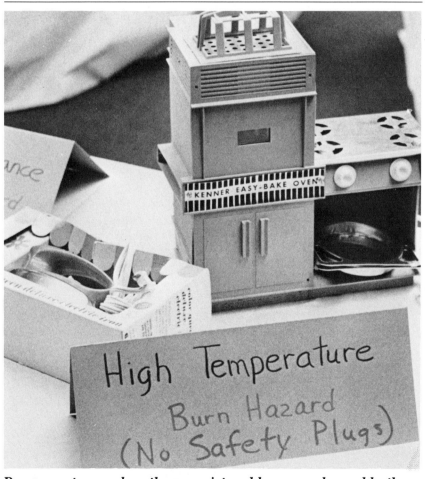

Dangerous toys, such as the oven pictured here, were banned by the FDA's Bureau of Product Safety (transferred in 1973 to the new Consumer Product Safety Commission). The Child Protection Act of 1966 prohibited the sale of all toys found to be hazardous to children.

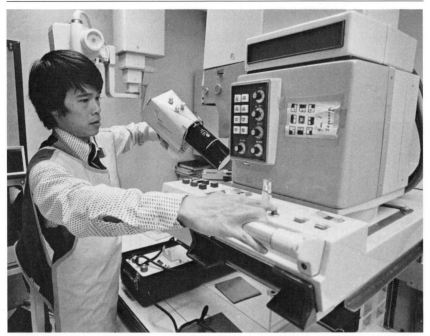

A radiation protection specialist operates a meter to detect harmful leaks around an X-ray viewing machine. The FDA was authorized in 1968 by the Radiation Health and Safety Act to regulate radiation-emitting devices.

persons suffering from various illnesses. This has, in fact, been an especially sensitive issue for the agency since its inception.

Though the FDA wants to make absolutely sure that every drug allowed on the market is safe and will produce no serious long-term effects, there are patients suffering from painful or lethal diseases who would try almost anything to alleviate or cure their ailment. What is the FDA to do? Approve a drug and then *hope* that no disaster will result? Or steadfastly stick to rules and regulations developed over nearly a century of protecting American consumers?

Complicating matters even further is the fact that many drug companies are highly reluctant to spend millions of dollars on research and development of a new drug without knowing whether the FDA will approve release of their product.

A partial answer to this problem was the passage of the Orphan Drug Act in 1983. Under FDA regulations, an orphan drug is defined as a drug intended for

46

a rare disease or condition "which occurs so infrequently in the United States that there is no reasonable expectation that the cost of developing and making available in the United States a drug for such disease or condition will be recovered from sales in the United States of such drug." This law allows manufacturers of products designated by the FDA as orphan drugs to take tax credits to cover the costs of developing and testing them. The law further encourages drug research by giving pharmaceutical companies seven years of exclusive rights to market products that are not normally patentable.

In 1985, the FDA took steps to speed up its drug-approval procedures by issuing a new set of agency regulations. These included measures requiring that any negative reactions to approved drugs be immediately reported to the FDA by drug manufacturers and doctors who prescribe them.

An example that illustrates the frustrations in clearing new drugs was the FDA's approval in 1987 of a clinically beneficial anti-AIDS (Acquired Immune

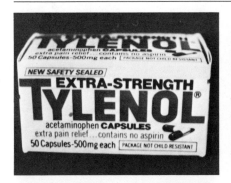

After a number of consumers had been fatally poisoned in 1982 by Extra-Strength Tylenol capsules laced with cyanide, the FDA required new safety-sealed and tamper-resistant packaging for all nonprescription drugs.

47

A biochemical engineer inspects machinery during production of the drug interferon. (Interferon protects noninfected cells against viruses.) The Orphan Drug Act of 1983 provides incentives for manufacturers to develop and market drugs to treat diseases, such as AIDS.

Deficiency Syndrome) drug, azidothymidine, or AZT. Approval was issued in a relatively short period of time—four months. Hoping to reduce the spiraling death rate, the FDA initially allowed the drug to be given to AIDS patients who suffered from pneumocystis carinii, a potentially deadly form of pneumonia seen only in advanced stages of the disease. Although officials stressed that AZT was not a cure for AIDS, patients wanted the drug regardless of what its limitations were thought to be. Since approval of the drug, it has now been established that AZT has serious side effects.

Many demonstrations against the federal government and the sole manufacturer of AZT have occurred to loosen up the drug's restrictive distribution and to cut the high cost to consumers who desire the medication (average cost to a patient is $10,000 a year). However, the FDA has been able to resist much public pressure to approve promising but largely untested drugs. But what of the future? As long as Americans die of disease, especially cancer and AIDS, there is likely to be continued pressure from both the government and the private sector for quicker approval of drugs that offer even the remotest chance for cure.

Clearly, the FDA has a responsibility to speedily approve drugs needed for treating diseases. But the agency must also ensure the safety of these drugs; that is the FDA's past objective and will probably continue to be into the foreseeable future.

A consumer safety officer checks a shipment of imported bananas to make sure they meet U.S. safety standards.

FOUR

Structure of the FDA

Today, the FDA bears little semblance to Wiley's tiny operation run out of the Department of Agriculture's basement many years ago. It presently employs nearly 7,000 men and women and operates on a budget of more than $480 million. It is one part of a much larger organization—the U.S. Department of Health and Human Services, located in Washington, D.C.

The FDA is managed by a commissioner who supervises a number of agency offices and centers that carry out the agency's major objective, consumer protection. A deputy commissioner and eight associate commissioners assist the commissioner and oversee the administration of the FDA from offices in Washington and in nearby Rockville, Maryland. The offices they direct are the Office of Management and Operations, the Office of Health Affairs, the Office of Science, the Office of Legislative Affairs, the Office of Planning and Evaluation, the Office of Public Affairs, the Office of Consumer Affairs, and the Office of Regulatory Affairs.

Agency Offices

The Office of Management and Operations advises the commissioner on all phases of management including the budget, personnel, and organization of the agency. It distributes the resources for funding programs, manpower, facilities, and equipment to the appropriate departments. The office also creates the

51

***An FDA chemist analyzes food samples for insect and animal
contamination.***

procedures used to safeguard trade secrets and other confidential information
submitted by industry to the FDA.

The Office of Health Affairs develops agency policies for medical research
projects and evaluates results of projects originating in other governmental
agencies and private institutions for potential use by the FDA. The Office of
Health Affairs represents the FDA on task forces, committees, and before
Congress on issues concerning medical policies, program direction, and the
goals of the agency. It also serves as the focal point for the coordination of
specific health-oriented projects—for instance, those related to approval of
new products that have significant impact on health-care practices in the United
States.

The Office of Science studies and evaluates quality-control programs (activities designed to assure adequate quality in procedures and products) in FDA laboratories. It also represents the FDA in its dealings with other federal, state, and local agencies, industries, universities, consumer organizations, scientific organizations, and Congress on matters involving science policy.

The Office of Legislative Affairs works with the commissioner's office, other officials at the Department of Health and Human Services, Congress, and the federal Office of Management and Budget to prepare and analyze data for congressional testimony on proposed or pending food and drug legislation. It also provides responses to important correspondence from Congress and consumers.

The Office of Planning and Evaluation reviews proposed FDA projects and programs and their funding sources and then prepares long-term planning strategies for the agency. The office also studies the impact of FDA programs on consumers.

A consumer safety officer weighs a box of cereal (left) to check a consumer's complaint about its contents.

The Office of Public Affairs furnishes the press and public with general information about the FDA. It publishes periodicals such as *FDA Consumer, FDA Today*, and the *FDA Drug Bulletin*, all of which keep consumers apprised of research, standards, and current programs regarding food, drugs, and cosmetics. The *FDA Enforcement Report* is published weekly and contains the latest information about product recalls, seizures, and mislabeled products whose misuse could cause serious health problems.

The Office of Consumer Affairs coordinates agency information about public-interest issues, surveys consumers, and studies the impact consumer involvement has in resolving those issues.

The Office of Regulatory Affairs advises the commissioner on FDA regulations and compliance-related matters that have an effect on the development of

An inspector from the FDA's field investigations branch in Tucson, Arizona, takes a careful look at watermelons from Mexico waiting to be cleared by U.S. Customs. At the border station, customs officers, Department of Agriculture inspectors, and FDA inspectors work together to check produce for possible contamination by insects, filth, and pesticides.

policy. It coordinates agency efforts to make sure industry complies with the regulations, including the standards for use of pesticides and chemicals. The Office of Regulatory Affairs prepares all the information describing the FDA's organization, its statement of policy, and methods of operation published in the *Federal Register*, a U.S. government publication that, by law, must include a description of every public agency, all presidential proclamations, and executive orders. The office also directs an elaborate network of FDA field operations consisting of 6 regional field offices, 21 district offices, and 135 resident inspection posts throughout the country. (Posts handle investigations for areas that are a little larger in size than those covered by the district offices.) The department responsible for the field operations, called the Office of Regional Operations, comprises four distinct divisions: Federal-State Relations, Field Science, Field Investigations, and Emergency and Epidemiological (disease-related) Operations.

The Division of Federal-State Relations supervises three branches of its own: the State Services Branch, the State Program Coordination Branch, and the State Training Branch. This division conducts several major activities:

1. Maintains the latest information on state laws that pertain to products regulated by the FDA.

2. Commissions state and local officials to help carry out federal activities such as inspections.

3. Continually updates the *State Inspector's Manual*, a guidebook used by the agency's many investigators and inspectors.

4. Manages the National Regional State Telecommunications Network. This is an electronic mail system in which computers link state food and drug agencies with the FDA regional field offices, district offices, and headquarters. The network can be of great value during emergencies—product recalls, for example—when quick and decisive action is crucial.

5. Conducts training and education programs for state, local, and federal employees.

The Division of Field Science also supervises three branches: the Mexican Liaison Staff, the Field Compliance Branch, and the Field Investigations Branch. This division has the following duties:

1. Coordinates all communication and activities between FDA and Mexican authorities relating to imported food and drugs.

2. Maintains training programs for Mexican officials to make sure that bilingual (English- and Spanish-speaking) officials are available on both sides of the border.

3. Prepares emergency plans with other governments in case of natural disasters, such as earthquakes and floods, that could affect food supply.

4. Controls the contents of the manuals and guidance materials used by FDA workers in the field.

5. Handles many of the day-to-day problems faced by FDA field inspectors and investigators. Such problems may be as minor as a lack of paper supplies or as serious as what to do about a sudden outbreak of disease.

Memoranda of Understanding

Another key element in the workings of the FDA is official agreements called Memoranda of Understanding. These are contracts between the FDA and state authorities, other federal agencies, and foreign governments in which areas of possible confusion are clarified; for example, an agreement with Canada that outlines the responsibilities of the FDA and Canada when shellfish from Canada is distributed in the United States. Most Memoranda of Understanding relate to the quality and safety of food.

The federal agencies that sign Memoranda of Understanding with the FDA include the departments of Agriculture, Commerce, and Defense and the Veterans Administration. Many of the agreements define the procedures for inspecting food products and establishments. Memoranda of Understanding help the FDA keep careful control over certain imported food products. Some of the methods used by the FDA to enforce these agreements are

1. *Customs Review of Invoices*. When a shipment arrives at a large customs port, an official of the U.S. Customs Service (a part of the Treasury Department) carefully reviews the entry documents to see if any food products are included. If there are, he or she notifies the local FDA inspector who then decides whether to make an on-site inspection or order a sample analysis. The U.S. Customs Service eventually makes the decision to admit or detain the shipment based on the FDA's report.

2. *Sample Analyses*. Both the FDA and the Bureau of Customs do sample testings. The FDA is mainly interested in the cleanliness or adulteration of the shipment. Customs is concerned with the percentage of certain ingredients to determine what tax rate to charge the distributor.

3. *Mobile Laboratories*. Very often, FDA laboratories become overloaded with sample analyses sent in by district inspectors. Part of this problem has been solved by the creation of small mobile labs. The mobile labs make it easier for samples to be taken and tested at the dock, thus freeing the analyst at the FDA laboratory for other duties.

A desolate street in Mexico City, photographed after an earthquake rocked the area in 1985. The Division of Field Science in the Office of Regional Operations assists foreign governments in protecting food supplies during emergencies.

4. *Ship-to-Ship Coverage.* This technique requires that an FDA inspector be at the point of discharge, such as a pier or airport, to examine the cargo as it is taken off the carrier. Such visual observation allows the FDA to inspect many more suspect imports than is possible using the Review of Invoices technique.

5. *Circuit Rider Program.* This program involves regular visits by FDA inspectors to remote ports. These visits are never prescheduled. Usually, such ports are "specialized," meaning that they handle only one or two types of food products. The program improves relations between FDA inspectors and foreign customs officials and allows agency inspectors to advise foreign officials on current problems.

6. *Inspection of Foreign Plants and Products.* Sometimes, companies overseas will formally request that the FDA inspect their plants and products in order to gain approval for distributing their products in the United States. These companies must pay all the costs of the FDA inspection.

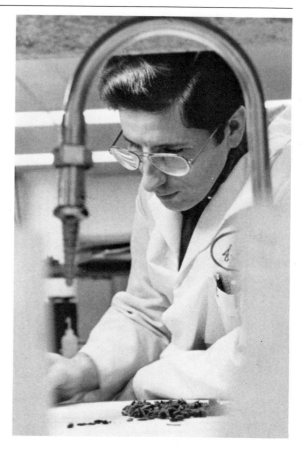

An FDA scientist in the district office in New York City analyzes a sample of the herb anise from Singapore for signs of insects or other filth.

Although the legal requirements that must be observed are the same for imported and domestic products, the enforcement procedures are different. If imported shipments do not comply with regulations, they can be held by U.S. Customs until they meet FDA standards. They can also be destroyed or sent back.

Agency Centers

The FDA carries out its activities through 6 centers and a field staff of investigators, scientists, and consumer affairs officers employed in 150 locations across the country. The centers study the problems in various food, drug, and cosmetic industries and employ experts in the fields of chemistry, microbiology, microanalysis (chemical analysis on a minute scale that requires special equipment), pharmacology, and human and veterinary medicine. These experts investigate harmful ingredients in food and drug samples and examine new techniques for processing, packaging, and storing foods and drugs.

The Center for Drug Evaluation and Research establishes standards for the safety, effectiveness, and labeling of prescription drugs and over-the-counter medications. It conducts clinical tests (tests on human patients) of new drugs before they can be approved for the market, and it regulates drugs already being sold by inspecting production facilities to make sure they comply with the law.

The Center for Biologics Evaluation and Research controls the standards for safety, effectiveness, and labeling of biological products (including serums, vaccines, toxins, antitoxins, and skin test substances) and human blood and its

A consumer safety officer looks into the sight glass of a fermentation tank in a Japanese factory. The FDA inspects foreign plants before they are allowed to sell their products in the United States.

An operator oversees an aspirin tablet press at the Bayer Company in Myerstown, Pennsylvania. The Center for Drug Evaluation and Research endorsed (under a physician's care) the use of an aspirin every other day to prevent repeated heart attacks in high-risk individuals.

FDA engineers measure an artificial knee joint (in the black box on the left) to check its surface roughness. Medical equipment and implants are tested at the Center for Medical Devices and Radiological Health.

derivatives. It also registers and inspects blood banks, licenses and inspects manufacturers of biological products, and conducts research on the development of biological products.

The Center for Food Safety and Applied Nutrition sets the standards for safe food and food-and-color additives and promotes safe cosmetics through research and regulatory actions.

The Center for Medical Devices and Radiological Health monitors medical devices intended for human use such as heart pacemakers, heating pads, and joint implants to assure their safety and effectiveness. It also collects information about problems with devices from manufacturers, the medical community, and consumers. It studies the biological effects of radiation exposure, designs methods to measure and control radiation emissions from devices such as x-ray machines, microwave ovens, and color televisions, and conducts consumer education programs to reduce public exposure to known radiation hazards.

The Center for Veterinary Medicine reviews and regulates veterinary preparations (drugs for animals), animal feed additives, and devices for animal use. It tries to ensure that drugs, such as antibiotics, used in food-producing animals do not threaten the health of human consumers.

The National Center for Toxicological Research, located in Jefferson, Arkansas (the only FDA center not located in the Washington, D.C., area), carries out research on the basic biological processes through which poisonous chemicals can harm the health of living organisms. FDA scientists can deduce from data obtained in research and tests performed on laboratory animals what possible effects the poisons will have on humans.

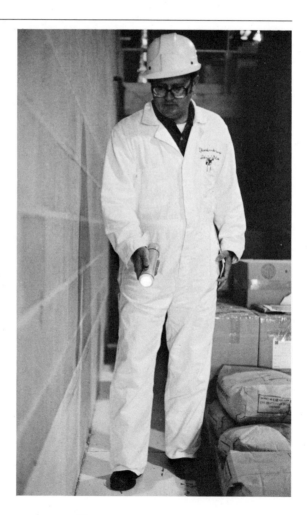

A consumer safety officer, flashlight in hand, examines a fish packing plant's storeroom seeking signs of rodents or insects. In 1987, the FDA made 20,298 inspections within the United States.

District Offices

Twenty-one district offices, under the Office of Regulatory Affairs, are considered the basic field operating units within the FDA. The district office usually has five major responsibilities at the local level: consumer affairs, investigative operations (inspections), enforcement of regulations, laboratory analyses of samples, and supervision of all FDA programs for the community.

The FDA supports a vast array of offices and laboratories to check the quality of foods, drugs, devices, and cosmetics. It must review thousands of applications for new products each year and regulate these products when they have been approved. The FDA must also respond to consumer complaints about products in an efficient manner and work with industry to eliminate harmful or questionable practices. The various offices' safety programs and the work of dedicated FDA scientists and inspectors form the backbone of the agency.

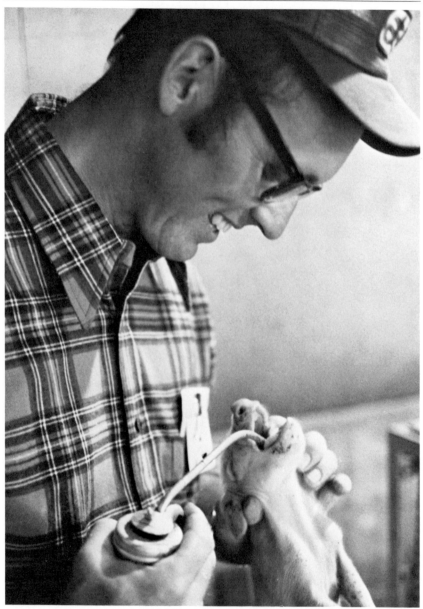

A farmer treats a pig with antibiotics to prevent internal infection. Prescription and nonprescription drugs for animals intended for human consumption must comply with FDA standards for safety and effectiveness.

FIVE

Investigation and Food Standards

The FDA is the federal government's primary consumer protection agency in matters relating to food, drugs, and cosmetics. It acts under laws passed by the U.S. Congress, most of which also apply to foreign products. The FDA works in close harmony with the U.S. Customs Service to make sure that all imported products meet required standards.

The FDA's major activities are as follows:

1. Makes periodic inspections of food processing plants and takes samples of their products to check for adulteration and mislabeling.

2. Establishes standards of identity and quality for food products.

3. Develops and enforces food labeling laws.

4. Helps the food industry to comply with the law and issues regulations designed to prevent violations.

5. Regulates drugs and feed given to animals to be used as food for humans.

6. Decides on the safety of food additives and determines when and how they may be used.

7. Enforces the limits on how much pesticide may remain on food crops, if any.

8. Determines the safety of food colors.

9. Warns the public when it uncovers a dangerous food product.

65

10. Carefully watches the nation's food supply to check for possible contamination with industrial chemicals and other dangerous substances.

11. Works closely with state authorities and other federal agencies during crises (earthquakes, fires, floods, etc.) to prevent widespread food and water contamination.

12. Initiates court proceedings against companies and persons violating the food and drug laws.

13. Works to ensure that drugs are safe, effective, and properly labeled.

14. Decides whether a drug can be sold over the counter or only with a doctor's prescription.

15. Decides whether or not prescription drug advertisements are misleading

In 1970, FDA Commissioner Charles Edwards testifies before the Senate Small Business Subcommittee in support of the requirement that drugmakers include a leaflet with their products telling of known and suspected hazards and side effects.

An FDA bacteriologist uses an automatic colony counter to determine the number of bacteria in a food sample.

or fraudulent. (The Federal Trade Commission has primary responsibility for nonprescription drug ads.)

16. Works to ensure that cosmetics are safe and properly packaged and labeled.

The functions and powers of the FDA are far-reaching and immense. It should be noted, however, that there are major restrictions on just what this agency can and *cannot* do. For example

1. It *cannot* regulate food manufacturers or businesses involved in commerce only within a single state. A Wisconsin sausage maker selling hot dogs and salami only to people within that state would not be subject to FDA regulations. It is up to the state of Wisconsin to oversee these products.

2. It *cannot* regulate sanitation facilities at individual restaurants, delicatessens, drive-in theaters, fast-food counters, etc. Again, this is a responsibility left to the individual states.

An employee in a mail-order drug firm sorts packages to be mailed to customers. Drugs sold by mail must be approved by the FDA prior to marketing.

3. It *cannot* regulate food prices and advertising. Food advertising is regulated by the Federal Trade Commission; however, if claims appear on the product's label rather than in an ad, the FDA is responsible for regulation.

4. It *cannot* regulate cigarettes. The Treasury Department's Bureau of Alcohol, Tobacco, and Firearms monitors the cigarette industry.

5. It *cannot* regulate food products sold through the mail, even if they are deceptive or fraudulent. That responsibility rests with the U.S. Postal Service.

Inspection

Of the many diverse functions of the FDA probably none is as complex or as challenging as that of actually enforcing the law. This is the principal duty of the FDA's inspectors, called consumer safety officers (CSOs). On any given day, they might be found at a dockside, making sure that a cargo of imported lamb complies with U.S. regulations; at a candy manufacturing plant to ensure sanitary conditions; at a court of law, testifying against a baby-food manufacturer whose product lacked adequate nutritional content; at a private home, listening to complaints about an electronic device that might have caused an illness; or in a supermarket or drugstore, buying products for testing in FDA laboratories.

When a CSO is given an assignment to inspect food production, storage facilities, or distribution of products, he or she goes over the FDA's guidelines and enforcement programs for the specific assignment. The agency publishes and updates three important publications for the CSO: the *Inspector Operations Manual*, the *Inspector Training Manual*, and the *Inspector's Technical Guide*.

A consumer safety officer (right) consults a drug company official while she inspects the drug plant to make sure its products are safe to use.

The CSO investigates the previous record of the company to see whether there have been any violations or consumer complaints in the past. From this preliminary investigation, the officer can learn much about the company's product and its method of operation.

Before visiting a facility, the CSO reviews a checklist of equipment needed for the on-site inspection. Often this list includes a flashlight to examine poorly lit areas, a set of portable scales to weigh products, a black ultraviolet light to check for rodent contamination (the light makes rodent urine glow brightly), a camera to document violations, sterile sieves and spoons to collect samples, and clean protective clothing and gear.

The CSO arrives at the plant unannounced. The Federal Food, Drug, and Cosmetic Act authorizes the CSO to enter any establishment at "a reasonable time, within a reasonable limit, and in a reasonable manner." The CSO must

Workers at a peach canning plant in California sort peaches along a conveyor. One of the tasks of consumer safety officers is to inspect the handling of peaches before they are sealed in cans.

simply present an identification badge. If the company being inspected refuses to allow the CSO entry, the CSO may return with an inspection warrant obtained in a federal court.

Once inside the plant, the officer invites the company's management to assign someone to accompany him throughout the inspection. The CSO carefully examines the raw materials used in the company's manufacturing— how they are received, handled, and stored—to see whether what the government defines as "filth" has contaminated a process or product. "Filth" includes "contaminants such as rat, mouse and other animal hairs and excreta, whole insects, insect parts and excreta, parasitic worms, pollution from the excrement of man and animals, as well as other extraneous materials" that, because of their repulsiveness, would not knowingly be eaten or used. Filth renders foods adulterated, whether or not a danger to health can be shown.

The CSO also examines a plant's construction and design and inspects everything from the location of lighting and washing equipment to devices that make sure no animals can enter the plant. Sanitary conditions, including clean water sources, sanitizing solutions, sewage disposal systems, and pesticide controls are inspected. The CSO checks for posted signs that instruct employees to wash their hands after using the lavatory.

The handling and storage of all raw materials, the legal use of food and color additives, the cleanliness of processing equipment, and the methods used to avoid contamination of food by biological and chemical means are all reviewed by the CSO. Controls regulating water pressure and temperature, humidity, sterilization, and refrigeration in the plant are also carefully observed. The CSO may take product samples for FDA analysis, but the law requires that a receipt be given to the company, which is also encouraged to make its own sample analysis. The FDA must promptly send a copy of the analysis result to the company.

Following a plant inspection, the CSO and plant management meet to discuss any violations and required corrections. Although the CSO usually insists that violations be corrected as soon as possible, he does not tell the company exactly how to make the changes. The officer prepares a "Report of Observations," which includes all details of findings, test results, samples collected, and any photographs of detected violations, and submits it to the FDA district office.

After the FDA district office has reviewed the report, it takes action against any violations. A letter is sent to the company asking what it plans to do about the violations. It is given 10 days to respond, and if violations continue, the FDA has a number of law-enforcement tools at its disposal, such as publicity,

71

In 1986, a drugstore employee removes boxes of Tylenol capsules from the shelf after a woman in New York died after taking cyanide-tainted Tylenol. Although the drug was in a tamper-resistant package, as a precaution, it was recalled, or removed, from the market during the investigation of her death.

information and regulatory letters, product recalls, product seizures, injunctions, and prosecution.

The Federal Food, Drug, and Cosmetic Act gives the FDA the power to publicize its administrative and legal actions; it is one of the few government agencies that has such authority. As a result, it publishes its *FDA Consumer* reports summarizing all seizures and criminal and injunction proceedings.

The FDA is also specifically authorized to publish information regarding food that is dangerous to the health of or seriously deceptive to consumers. This information is published in the weekly *FDA Enforcement Report*, which lists all of that week's cases of prosecution, seizures, injunctions, and recalls. The

FDA also publicizes its activities through news conferences, press releases, articles in private journals, special consumer education conferences, and speeches by its employees.

Information and regulatory letters are also used by the FDA to enforce the law. An information letter is sent to a firm if the FDA suspects that the label on one of its products does not meet the prescribed requirements. This is considered a minor violation, and the FDA allows approximately 30 days for a company to respond.

A regulatory letter is stronger than an information letter. It advises a firm that it may have violated one or more provisions of the Food, Drug, and Cosmetic Act. The letter also states that corrective actions must be taken to avoid court action. A company receiving a regulatory letter is given 10 days to respond.

The FDA uses the regulatory letter when it feels that a violation has not been intentional and when a company has no past record of similar violations. All regulatory letters are a matter of public record and can be examined by interested citizens.

When a product poses a threat to public safety, immediate action is necessary. All FDA-regulated products can be removed from the market by means of a recall. A recall requires a company to remove a defective or dangerous product in order to correct it, if possible. The product may be reissued to consumers when corrected or the manufacturer may provide a refund or item exchange. Recalls can also be voluntarily undertaken by a manufacturer to carry out its responsibility to protect consumers from adulterated products. The FDA's role is primarily one of monitoring the recall and the corrective action to be taken on the recalled products.

The FDA uses three classes of recalls. A Class 1 recall involves situations where a consumer's use of, or exposure to, a product will probably cause serious health problems. An example of a Class 1 recall is a situation involving misbranding of a drug, perhaps by recommending improper dosage. A Class 2 recall involves products that may cause the consumer to suffer temporary or treatable health problems. Food poisoning from eating decomposed shrimp is one example. A Class 3 recall is a situation in which a consumer's use of, or exposure to, a product is not likely to have damaging effects—for instance, when a tube of antibiotic ointment is packaged in a box made for another product by the same company.

Seizure, another action taken by the FDA to protect consumers, involves confiscation of a select lot of goods alleged to be in violation and to remove it from commerce. Seizure actions might be taken against goods containing nonapproved food additives, misbranded products, or goods that weigh less than their stated weight. The FDA initiates a seizure by filing a complaint with the U.S. district court where the goods are located. A U.S. marshal is then directed by the court to take possession of the goods until the matter is settled. The owner of the seized merchandise usually has about 30 days to decide on a course of action. He may do nothing, in which case the goods will be disposed of by the court; he may ask the court for time to bring his product into compliance with the law; or he may decide to fight the government and press for a trial.

The FDA also relies on injunctions to help enforce the law. Injunctions are civil actions filed by the FDA against a person or company. Usually they represent attempts by the agency to stop a company from continuing to manufacture a product in violation of the law. As with seizures, however, injunctions can involve lengthy and complicated court battles with no certainty that the FDA's case will be upheld.

Criminal prosecution is the final and most extreme action the FDA can take against a business, and it decides to prosecute only after detailed and careful consideration. The agency reviews a number of issues before prosecuting a company:

1. Is the violation serious?
2. Is the violation intentional?
3. Will prosecution make the company act more responsibly in the future?
4. Does the agency have enough evidence to bring about a successful prosecution?
5. Will prosecution benefit consumers of this particular industry's products?
6. Does the company have repeated violations on its record or has it fought past FDA attempts to enforce the law?
7. Are the company's violations gross or flagrant, such as molds and animal excrement on or in food products?
8. Do the violations threaten life or cause injuries? Botulism from improperly canned food products might be one such example.
9. Do the violations involve outright fraud? Submitting false records or deliberately lying about the package weight of a product would fall into this category.

When the file of a recommended prosecution is reviewed by various offices within the FDA, every attempt is made to make sure the review is fair and unbiased. Lawyers for both the FDA and the Department of Justice go over all the case's details to ensure that there is enough evidence to justify filing a suit with the court.

Two other aspects of enforcing the food and drug laws should be mentioned. First, the FDA will not prosecute a person or company simply on technical grounds, for example, if a label on a can of tomato paste mistakenly reads "40 oz." instead of "4 oz.": clearly a typographical error. Although the error represents a grossly fraudulent statement, the FDA would never think of prosecuting such a case. Once informed of the mistake, the company would simply recall all the mislabeled cans and apply new labels to them. Second, the FDA does not prosecute a corporation only. Specific individuals will be charged because a company alone cannot commit a crime. These persons must be in a responsible position within the company, have knowledge of the violation, and have the power to correct it but appear to have failed to do so.

Food Standards

To protect consumers from being cheated by inferior products and fraudulent labels, the FDA has issued three kinds of food standards: standards of identity, standards of quality, and standards of fill of containers.

Standards of identity define exactly what a given food product is and determine which ingredients the food must contain. They specify the correct

Two brothers make peanut butter sandwiches. The food on the left meets FDA standards and can therefore be called by common names: "milk," "ice cream," "enriched bread," "preserves," and "peanut butter." The food on the right does not meet FDA standards because of substituted ingredients and cannot be called by common names; for example, the Smucker's product is called "strawberry spread" instead of "strawberry preserves."

The mandatory label information on canned cut green beans (center and right) includes the identity of the product, "green beans," a description of their appearance, "cut," a list of the ingredients in the order of their predominance by weight, and the name and address of the distributor as well as optional information such as the universal product code.

name of the food and other required label information (for example, orange drink is not orange juice). Standards of identity limit the amount of water permitted in the food, define the kind and amount of certain vitamins and minerals that must be present in food labeled "enriched," and set the required amounts of expensive ingredients and limits on the inexpensive ones.

Standards of quality are minimum standards for canned fruits and vegetables. They set up quality requirements for characteristics such as color, ripeness, and tenderness. These standards protect consumers from such products as mushy carrots, hard corn, or stewed tomatoes with too much core and peel in the can.

Standards of fill of containers indicate how full a can, box, or package must be to avoid misleading the prospective buyer. If a food falls below a standard issued by the FDA it must clearly have stamped on its label: "BELOW STANDARD IN FILL."

The FDA has established standards for hundreds of foods. Specifications are extremely detailed and precise. For example, the standard of fill specifications for canned peas reads:

> *Fill of container*—(1) The standard of fill of container for canned peas is a fill such that, when the peas and liquid are removed from the container and returned thereto, the leveled peas (irrespective of the quantity of the liquid), 15 seconds after they are so returned completely fill the container. A container with lid attached by double seam shall be considered to be completely filled when it is filled to the level 3/16 inch vertical distance below the top of double seam. . . .

FDA regulations regarding food packaging and labeling are just as exacting and extensive as those for food standards. The only foods that do not fall under FDA guidelines are meats and poultry, which are regulated by the U.S. Department of Agriculture. However, soups containing small amounts of meat, poultry, or broth as flavoring ingredients are subject to FDA regulation.

The information on the label of a food package is categorized into mandatory information, mandatory wordings of certain information, and optional information. Mandatory information tells the consumer what form the food product is in. Such terms as *sliced, whole,* or *chopped* may indicate how a consumer can expect to find the product prepared for consumption. The quantity of food in the package—its weight, measure, number of items, or a combination of these categories—is considered mandatory information and must be provided on the package label. The food's ingredients must be listed in the order of predominance by weight and the presence of any artificial coloring or chemical preservative must be included. If the label indicates that a certain number of servings can be obtained from the contents of a package, the size of each serving must also be indicated. The food must be identified by its commonly used name in addition to its brand name on the package. The name and address of the manufacturer, packer, or distributor must also appear on the label.

Mandatory labeling of certain other information is required under special circumstances. For example, nutritional labeling is ordinarily voluntary, but it becomes mandatory when a nutrient is *added* to the product (such as vitamin C to fruit drinks and vitamin D to skim milk). Another situation in which mandatory labeling applies is one in which statements about savings to the consumer are made. If the sponsor of a food product includes such a label, the wording must comply with special regulations. For instance, the container may represent economy by virtue of its size ("economy size," "thrifty pack," or "bargain size"). If the label has words to this effect, the FDA requires that the sponsor must offer, at the same time, the same brand of that product in at least one smaller size. And the economy package's price must be at least five percent less than the price per weight or volume of the smaller package.

Optional information includes such things as a universal product code (a computerized code for checkout and inventory), special symbols (the letter K inside the letter O indicates that a food is kosher and thus complies with Jewish dietary laws), a suggested recipe, storage and cooking instructions, games, or competitions—none of which is authorized or regulated by the FDA.

The FDA has also issued regulations for certain items that are not easily definable as food, and yet are classified as such; products such as gelatin and bottled water are but two examples. Frozen "heat and serve" dinners also fall into this category. The FDA specifies that frozen dinners contain at least three components: one or more sources of protein derived from meat, fish, poultry, cheese, or eggs; one or more vegetables or vegetable mixtures other than potatoes, rice, or a cereal-based product; and potatoes, rice, a cereal-based

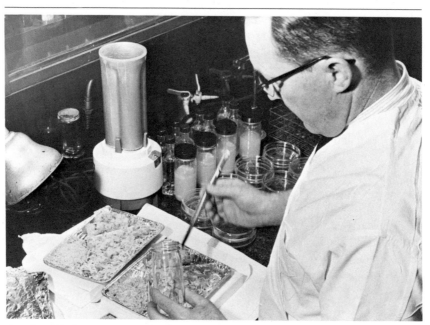

A microbiologist examines the contents of a frozen dinner. The FDA has established standards for the ingredients of such dinners. They must include at least one source of protein, one vegetable, and potatoes, rice, or a cereal-based product.

product (other than bread or rolls), or another vegetable or vegetable mixture. The FDA also specifies that the sauces and gravies accompanying these foods contain a prescribed minimum amount of protein and nutrients.

Food and Color Additives

The use of food and color additives is an area of FDA regulation that has always attracted controversy. Since the 1960s, the safety of food additives has been closely watched by the public as well as by the FDA.

The first thing a food manufacturer must do if it wants to introduce a new chemical as a food additive is to file a petition with the FDA. The petition must include lengthy reports of investigations made to ensure the safety of the additive's usage, and it must include detailed data derived from experiments on animals. By law, it must not omit anything that might make the FDA take a negative view of the proposed chemical.

According to the Federal Food, Drug, and Cosmetic Act, if a chemical substance is legally a food additive then its use will be restricted. However, the law provides for an important exception: "A chemical substance will not be legally a food additive if it is 'generally recognized as safe (GRAS) under the conditions of intended use.' "

But how does the FDA determine whether a substance falls under the GRAS classification? This question has been the center of controversy for years. In general, the FDA follows this criterion: "If a chemical substance is a food ingredient of natural biological origin that has been widely consumed for its nutrient properties in the United States without detrimental effects," it most likely will receive a GRAS classification. There are approximately 700 additives that are considered GRAS, including flavoring agents such as spices.

The FDA requires that all color additives for food use must receive FDA safety clearance before the color can be marketed or used. The manufacturer is required to submit a sample of the color to the FDA for chemical analysis. After analysis, the FDA is authorized to specify the limitations or safe levels of the color additive. If a color additive is shown to be carcinogenic (cancer causing) in animals or humans, it is not permitted to be used in food.

Pesticides and chemical contaminants are another concern of the FDA. Although a pesticide is not technically a food additive it does appear in food for human consumption because of various harvesting and processing techniques. As a result, the Food, Drug, and Cosmetic Act requires that contaminant tolerances be established; these levels are set by the Environmental Protection Agency (EPA) and enforced by the FDA. Some of the most common pesticide chemicals for which safe limits have been set are captan, copper, diquat, hydrogen cyanide, and simazine.

One of the most troublesome food protection problems is the presence of "unintentional" chemical contaminants. Mercury in seafood, DDT (an insecticide) in a number of foods such as produce, lead in evaporated milk, and PCB (an environmental pollutant) in food packages are typical examples. The FDA has the power to remove chemically contaminated food from the market, but often does not have the time or money to do so. Also, it is unrealistic to ban all milk, fish, meat, and other foods when chemicals are present but in apparently harmless amounts. Again, the FDA works closely with the EPA in setting up safe tolerance levels. Only when the public's health is clearly at risk does the agency resort to legal action.

One major purpose of the nation's principal food and drug law is to ensure sanitation and wholesomeness in food manufacturing. One of the FDA's basic tools in this regard is the issuing of Good Manufacturing Practices (GMP) regulations. The GMP program began in 1969 when the FDA published its first such regulation. In general, these regulations, which are rigidly enforced by

Hogs being fed with corn on an Iowa farm. Tolerance levels of pesticides used on corn are established by the Environmental Protection Agency; however, the FDA enforces the regulation.

A worker supervises the assembly line at a can-making plant. Lead, a poisonous metallic element, is used to solder the seams of the tin cans. The FDA is working with industry to reduce the amount of lead that seeps into canned foods.

frequent inspections, make sure that all plant workers are conscientiously clean when working with or near food. They make sure that all equipment is as sterile as possible, that all food utensils are cleaned and sanitized before use, and that all water used in cleaning be adequately pure.

Since the beginning of the GMP program in 1969, the FDA has been periodically issuing new GMP regulations, each of which applies to a particular food industry. As science and technology develop at an ever-accelerating pace, the FDA's endeavors are likely to increase.

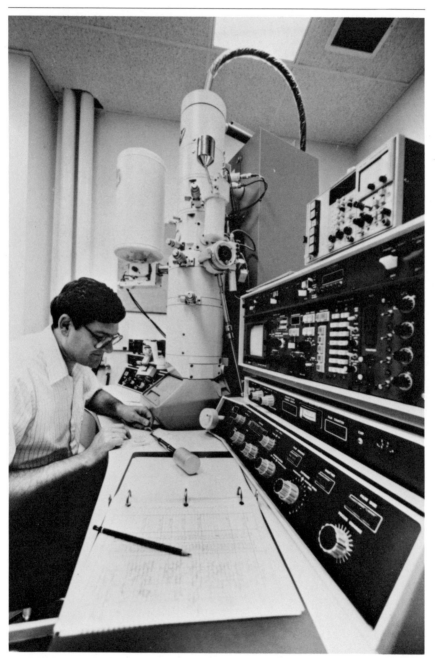

An FDA scientist tests an artificial heart valve to ensure its safety.

SIX

Eyes Toward the Future

Of all the many federal agencies, probably none affects us on a daily basis more than the Food and Drug Administration. In some respects this is ironic, because few Americans ever give the FDA a moment's thought. But within this irony is also a tribute to the quiet effectiveness with which the FDA goes about its business.

In January 1987, two disturbing articles about the FDA appeared in the *New York Times*. One suggested that the agency had become soft during the presidency of Ronald Reagan. The author of the article accused the administration of giving in to drug and corporate interests that want more rapid approval of new products. The author of the second article took an opposite stance and charged the FDA with needlessly holding up approval of promising new drugs, especially ones offering hope to the thousands suffering from AIDS. Some doctors are presently dispensing the FDA's quickly approved "pentamidine" to AIDS patients. Taken through the lungs by a mist-making device, this drug treats the life-threatening AIDS-related pneumonia called pneumocystis carinii (PCP). Permitted by the FDA for PCP only, at first, public pressure has coerced the FDA to distribute the drug to any AIDS patient who desires it, regardless of the type of opportunistic infection. "Guerrilla" (unlicensed) clinics are dispensing homemade versions of immuno-builder drugs such as egg-lipid (protein) mixtures.

At a press conference in June 1986, FDA Commissioner Dr. Frank Young discusses the FDA's approval of the drug interferon for use in treating a rare form of blood cancer.

What does the future hold for the FDA? Will it alter the conservative policies that have characterized it until now? Probably, at least with regard to AIDS, the FDA will be forced to speed up approval of drugs not thoroughly tested by time or science.

The FDA does not work alone in establishing and enforcing food and drug regulations. Physicians, scientists, manufacturers, Congress, and state and federal courts continually add their opinions and scientific findings to the controversial debate about industrial regulation in the United States. The FDA must constantly interact with these forces to form policies and procedures for the evaluation and approval of new products, and to monitor processors, packagers, and distributors to keep them within the law and attentive to the health and safety of the consumer.

Whatever the debate about the agency and its future, this much can be said about the FDA: Americans would be less safe and less healthy without it.

Food and Drug Administration
DEPARTMENT OF HEALTH AND HUMAN SERVICES

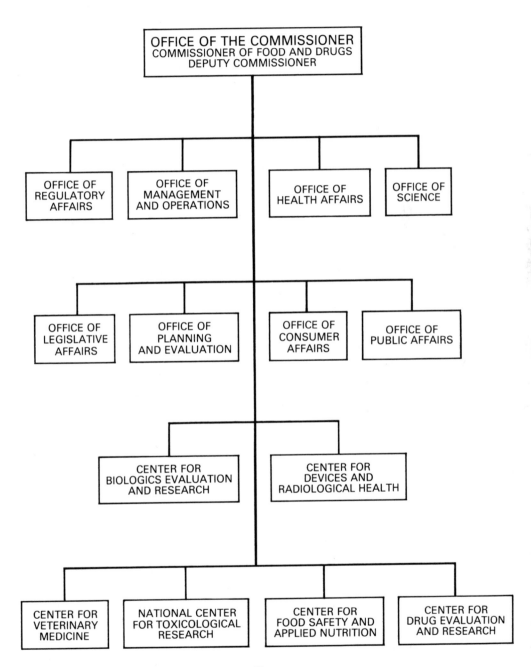

OFFICE OF THE COMMISSIONER
COMMISSIONER OF FOOD AND DRUGS
DEPUTY COMMISSIONER

OFFICE OF REGULATORY AFFAIRS

OFFICE OF MANAGEMENT AND OPERATIONS

OFFICE OF HEALTH AFFAIRS

OFFICE OF SCIENCE

OFFICE OF LEGISLATIVE AFFAIRS

OFFICE OF PLANNING AND EVALUATION

OFFICE OF CONSUMER AFFAIRS

OFFICE OF PUBLIC AFFAIRS

CENTER FOR BIOLOGICS EVALUATION AND RESEARCH

CENTER FOR DEVICES AND RADIOLOGICAL HEALTH

CENTER FOR VETERINARY MEDICINE

NATIONAL CENTER FOR TOXICOLOGICAL RESEARCH

CENTER FOR FOOD SAFETY AND APPLIED NUTRITION

CENTER FOR DRUG EVALUATION AND RESEARCH

GLOSSARY

Additives   Chemical substances added to food to increase its shelf life or to improve desirable properties such as flavor, color, and texture.

Adulterated Food   Food made impure by the addition of a foreign or inferior substance, or the substitution for or removal of an important ingredient.

Consumer Safety Officer (CSO)   An FDA inspector who is responsible for enforcing food and drug laws. CSOs inspect manufacturing plants and investigate consumer complaints.

Food Standards   FDA regulations that maintain the quality of products and fairness of the presentation of those products in the interest of the consumer.

Generally Recognized as Safe (GRAS)   An FDA classification used to distinguish food ingredients of natural biological origin from synthetic and unsafe food additives.

Good Manufacturing Practices (GMP)   FDA regulations that explain what is needed to maintain sanitary conditions in food manufacturing plants; for example, such matters as building design, lighting, and materials handling.

Information Letter   An FDA letter sent to a firm if the FDA suspects that the label on one of the firm's products does not meet FDA requirements.

Injunction   Civil action filed by the FDA against a person or company to stop the manufacture of products in violation of the law.

Memoranda of Understanding   Contracts between the FDA and state authorities, other federal agencies, and foreign governments, in which areas of possible confusion or overlap in enforcing regulations are clarified.

Misbranded   Describing a product's label bearing false or misleading statements or a package misrepresenting the amount of food contained within.

Pesticide   A chemical agent, used to destroy agricultural pests, that may turn up in food because of various harvesting and processing techniques.

Preservative   An additive used to protect against decay, discoloration, or spoilage.

Recall   An FDA order that requires a company to immediately remove a defective or dangerous product from the marketplace. A recall may also be initiated by a manufacturer voluntarily.

Regulatory Letter   An FDA letter sent to notify a person or company that they are in violation of a provision of the Federal Food, Drug, and Cosmetic Act and to outline corrective procedures that must be taken to avoid court action.

Seizure   A civil court action in which a select lot of goods is confiscated in order to protect consumers from a dangerous product.

Standards of Fill of Container   Precise standards set by the FDA that indicate how full a can, box, or package must be to avoid misleading the prospective buyer.

SELECTED REFERENCES

Anderson, Oscar E., Jr. *The Health of a Nation: Harvey W. Wiley and the Fight for Pure Food.* Chicago: University of Chicago Press, 1958.

Block, Zenas. *It's All on the Label: Understanding Food Additives and Nutrition.* Boston: Little, Brown, 1981.

Jackson, Charles O. *Food and Drug Legislation in the New Deal.* Princeton, NJ: Princeton University Press, 1970.

Janssen, Wallace F. "America's First Food and Drug Laws." *FDA Consumer,* June 1975.

————. "Outline of the History of U.S. Drug Regulation and Labeling." *Food, Drug, Cosmetic Law Journal,* August 1981, 420–441.

————. "The Story of the Laws Behind the Labels." *FDA Consumer,* June 1981, 32–45.

Jones, Claire, et al. *Pollution: The Food We Eat.* Minneapolis: Lerner Publications Co., 1974.

Kallet, Arthur, and F. J. Schlink. *One Hundred Million Guinea Pigs: Dangers in Everyday Foods, Drugs, and Cosmetics.* 1933. Reprint. Salem, NH: Ayer, 1976.

Lucas, Scott. *The FDA.* Millbrae, CA: Celestial Arts, 1978.

Neal, Harry E. *Protectors: The Story of the Food and Drug Administration.* New York: Julian Messner, 1968.

Temin, Peter. *Taking Your Medicine: Drug Regulation in the United States.* Cambridge, MA: Harvard University Press, 1980.

Turner, James S. *The Chemical Feast. Report on the Food and Drug Administration.* New York: Viking, 1970.

U.S. Department of Health and Human Services. *Requirements of Laws and Regulations Enforced by the U.S. Food and Drug Administration.* Washington, DC: U.S. Government Printing Office, 1984.

Wilson, J. Q. *The Politics of Regulation.* New York: Basic Books, 1982.

Young, James H. *The Toadstool Millionaires: A Social History of Patent Medicines in America Before Federal Regulation.* Princeton, NJ: Princeton University Press, 1972.

INDEX

William Patrick has worked for many years as an editor for New York publishers, specializing in reference works on American history and government. He has also edited the compilations of a major national public opinion poll.

Arthur M. Schlesinger, jr., served in the White House as special assistant to Presidents Kennedy and Johnson. He is the author of numerous acclaimed works in American history and has twice been awarded the Pulitzer Prize. He taught history at Harvard College for many years and is currently Albert Schweitzer Professor of the Humanities at the City College of New York.

PICTURE CREDITS:

AP/Wide World Photos: pp. 47, 48, 53, 60, 68; Food and Drug Administration: cover, pp. 24, 28, 37; Ellis Herwig: p. 70; Library of Congress: pp. 19, 20, 21, 22, 26, 27, 30, 31, 32, 34, 35, 40, 42, 52, 67, 78; Magnum Photos Inc., cover; Smithsonian Institution: p. 23; UPI/Bettmann Newsphotos: pp. 16, 41, 57, 72; Courtesy of USDA: cover, pp. 2, 14, 17, 43, 46, 50, 54, 58, 59, 61, 62, 64, 66, 69, 75, 76, 80, 81, 84; *Washington Post:* reprinted courtesy D.C. Public Library: pp. 38, 45.